Roberto Clemente

YOUNG BASEBALL HERO

Roberto Clemente

YOUNG BASEBALL HERO

By Francene Sabin and JoAnn Early Macken
Illustrated by Yoshi Miyake

SCHOLASTIC INC.
New York Toronto London Auckland Sydney
Mexico City New Delhi Hong Kong Buenos Aires

ISBN-13: 978-0-439-02023-7
ISBN-10: 0-439-02023-9

12 11 10 9 8 7 6 5   10 11 12 13/0

Printed in the U.S.A.
First printing, March 2008

CONTENTS

Let's Go   1

Home and Family   5

Workdays and Nights   13

Harvest Time   17

Baseball and a Bicycle   23

A Natural Athlete   33

Moving Up   40

Disaster and Loss   48

Index   53

CHAPTER 1:

"Let's Go!"

In August 1960, the Pittsburgh Pirates played the San Francisco Giants at Forbes Field in Pittsburgh. At the top of the seventh inning, the Pirates were ahead with a score of 1-0. But that was not much of a lead against such a hard-hitting team, especially with Willie Mays, the Giants' best hitter, up at bat.

The Pirates' pitcher whipped a fastball toward the plate. Mays swung and connected, sending the ball speeding toward the right-field wall. At the crack of bat against ball, the Pirates' right fielder, Roberto Clemente, whirled and raced toward the wall. Clemente's left arm reached up, and the ball smacked into his glove! But then Clemente smacked into the concrete wall. Blood dripped from a cut on his chin.

Clemente fell to his knees, stunned. He shook his head to clear it. Then he raised the glove, showing the white ball nestled in the brown leather pocket. The crowd went wild. *"Arriba! Arriba!"* thousands of Pittsburgh fans screamed. The jubilant cry followed him every step of the way back to the Pirates' dugout.

"*Arriba!*" is a Spanish word that means "Let's go!" A Pirates announcer started yelling it each time Roberto Clemente came to bat or made a great play. The hometown fans repeated it as a way of telling Roberto Clemente how much they loved him. Cheering him on in Spanish, the fans said something special to the great Puerto Rican-born ballplayer.

The hometown fans' approval was important to Roberto Clemente. Baseball was his life, and he wanted to be a perfect player every inning of every game. He was proud when he did well. He felt happy when his fans appreciated what he did for them.

After that famous catch, doctors stitched the cut in Roberto Clemente's jaw. He sat out five games while he waited for it to heal. The Pirates then went on to play in the World Series!

CHAPTER 2:
Home and Family

Roberto Clemente was born on August 18, 1934, in Puerto Rico. This sunny island is located between the North Atlantic Ocean and the Caribbean Sea. Puerto Rico is a territory of the United States, and people who live there are U.S. citizens. Like most people of the island, Roberto and his family spoke Spanish. The family was black, but that did not matter much in Puerto Rico. No laws prevented people of different races from eating together in restaurants, staying in the same hotels, dating, or marrying.

The Clemente family lived in a *barrio*, or neighborhood, called San Anton. San Anton was a section of a town called Carolina. Carolina, then part of the countryside, is about ten miles from San Juan, the capital of Puerto Rico.

When Roberto Clemente was a boy, San Anton had tiny, twisting streets dotted with small, modest houses. Everyone in the *barrio* was poor, but the district was not a slum. Like

those in the rest of Carolina, most of its people were hardworking laborers and shopkeepers.

The Clemente family's five-room wooden house had electricity and indoor plumbing. The family collected rainwater on the roof for drinking. Inside the house, the walls were plain white, and the simple furniture was made of wood.

Sugar cane provided the main source of employment for Carolina's citizens. They worked in the fields, planting, cutting, and gathering the cane. They loaded and drove

the wagons that carried the cane to processing plants. They worked in the plants, turning the crop into sugar to be shipped all over the world.

Melchor Clemente, Roberto's father, was a foreman in charge of a crew of sugar cane cutters. His job was to see that the men worked well and earned their pay. He also made sure

that the crew was treated fairly by the sugar company's management.

Melchor was a quiet, thoughtful, even-tempered man. The workers respected him. So did his family. Mr. Clemente's rules for living were firm. A man had dignity, an̶ cont̶ ̶ ̶ ̶d to the well-being of hi̶ A̶ ̶ ̶ ̶y mon̶ ̶ ̶ey he owed. A ̶ess fortunate than ̶d in hard work and ̶s family. ̶d he

Luisa Clemente, Roberto's mother, also set high standards. She was deeply religious, warmhearted, and devoted to her family. Together, Luisa and Melchor were wonderful ⬡nts to their children. Two of them, Luis Oquendo, were Luisa's children from ⬡. Their father died when they ⬡hor and Luisa Clemente ⬡ldo, Justino (also ⬡ Roberto.

Roberto never got to know his sister Anairis. He was still a baby when she died after being badly burned when gasoline spilled near an outdoor stove.

Roberto, the youngest, was a strong, healthy, handsome baby. His brother Matino remembered Roberto as a child. "Basically, Roberto was a good kid. He did two things—played ball and stayed home. He never got into trouble. He was always

quiet, never got spanked. We used to kid him about that."

Even as a child, Roberto liked to take his time to think things through. When someone called him, he often answered, "*Momentito.*" Just a minute. He said it so many times that his cousin started calling him "Momen." The name caught on and became a family nickname.

CHAPTER 3:
Workdays and Nights

Mr. and Mrs. Clemente worked long and hard to give their children a good home. In his job as foreman, Mr. Clemente earned only about five or ten dollars a week. That was not much money even then, so the Clementes did other work, too.

Mr. Clemente bought an old truck. He used it to haul sugar cane, sand and gravel for construction work, and building materials. He also carried meat and other food, which he sold in his spare time. He drove around

Carolina, stopping at houses to sell the food. His truck was like a traveling grocery store. Mr. Clemente also rented the truck to local merchants and businesses.

Mrs. Clemente earned money by doing laundry at the home of the owner of the sugar cane factory. But she did not like to leave her children during the day. So she woke up in the middle of the night and went to work while Mr. Clemente and the children slept. She also sewed and cooked for the cane cutters.

During the Great Depression, life was difficult in the barrio. Nobody had much money. Sugar cane was harvested from November until early summer. Most of the next year's crop was planted during the same months. The people of Carolina earned most of their small incomes during this time. But from midsummer until November, there was no work. It was called "*el tiempo muerto*," or "the dead time."

During "the dead time," people in the barrio survived by eating vegetables they grew in their gardens. Many families also kept chickens. The chickens supplied eggs and

meat. Fishing added variety to their daily diet.

Mr. Clemente did not rest during "the dead time." He sold food from his truck. Often his customers had no money to pay him. He thought it was important to help people who were less fortunate than he. He trusted them to pay their debts when they went back to work.

CHAPTER 4:

Harvest Time

In the barrio, the sugar cane harvest marked the beginning of each new year. Roberto always remembered how the cane fields looked, smelled, and felt. As a boy, he liked to walk with his mother to the cane fields each day when she brought Mr. Clemente his lunch.

To the boy, the fields were like a green forest. The ripe sugar cane stood nearly fifteen feet high, more than twice as tall as a grown man. The cane cutters moved through the fields in

straight lines. "Whoosh! Whoosh!" whispered their razor-sharp machetes as they chopped down row after row of stalks.

Workdays were long and tiring during the harvest season. People in the barrio woke up early, at five or six in the morning. By seven o'clock, the laborers had finished the breakfasts of rice and beans they had cooked the night before. They tied cords around the bottoms of their pant legs so the insects and snakes in the fields could not bite them. They put on broad straw hats and picked up their farm tools. Some workers gathered along the road and waited for trucks to take them out to the fields. Others walked to work.

Roberto's father sometimes rode a horse.

At about nine o'clock in the morning, the workers took a break for coffee and a piece of bread. Then the cutting started again. Roberto Clemente never forgot the words his father and the other men used to describe their labors. They spoke of "doing battle" with the cane, as if the sugar cane fields were their enemies in a never-ending war.

While the men worked in the fields, the women of Carolina spent part of the morning cooking hot meals

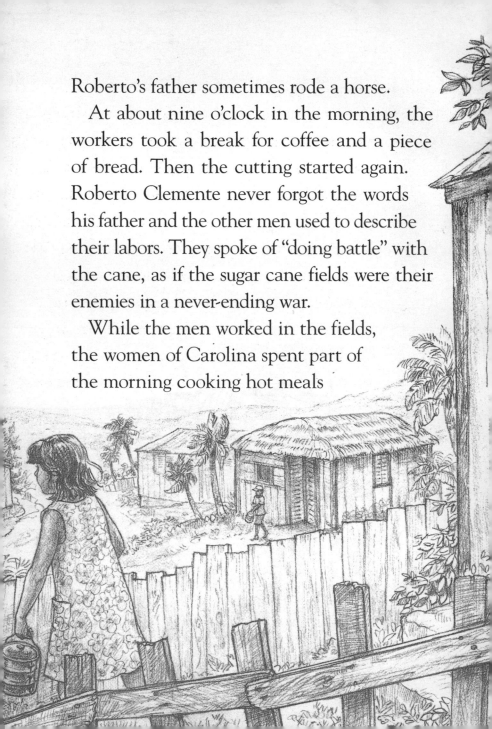

for them. Each woman put food into three or four pails. One pail might hold boiled green bananas or a stew made from potatoes, yams, or corn meal with bits of chicken or fish. A second container might be filled with rice. A third one could hold red or white beans in a sauce. Women and children carried the pails of food to the workers in the fields. At noon, the workers stopped for lunch.

The workday ended by four o'clock. The men came home, bathed, and shaved. After that, they had time to relax, listen to the radio, and play baseball.

CHAPTER 5:

Baseball and a Bicycle

Roberto was a good child, quiet and respectful. Only one thing led him to disobey or forget how to behave—baseball. Mrs. Clemente had to keep him inside when the family was getting ready to go somewhere. "I would dress him up, nice and clean," she said, "and Roberto would come home full of dust and mud. I'd send him to the store on an errand, and he'd be gone for hours." Mrs. Clemente did not worry too much about Roberto, though. She knew where to find him—outside in the street, playing baseball.

"When I was a little kid, the only thing I used to do was play ball all the time," Roberto said. "With a paper ball, with a rubber ball, with a tennis ball." He practiced hitting old tin cans and bottle caps with broomsticks.

"Roberto used to buy those rubber balls every chance he got," Mrs. Clemente said. "When he was small, he would lie in bed and bounce the ball off the walls. There were times he was so much in love with baseball that he did not care for food."

Roberto worked when he could. He was expected to earn his own spending money. So he did household chores. He helped his father load and unload the truck. He even earned a few pennies for bringing ice water to the workers cutting cane.

When he was nine years old, Roberto asked his parents for a bicycle. "If you want a bicycle, you will need to earn the money for it," Mr. Clemente told him.

Roberto looked for a way to earn the money for a bicycle. The answer came when a neighbor offered him a job. Roberto could earn a penny a day for carrying a milk can to the country store a half mile away, filling it, and bringing it back. Roberto agreed and did the task faithfully.

"Six o'clock every morning, I went for the milk," Clemente told a reporter years later. "I wanted to do it. I wanted to have work, to be a good man. I grew up with that on my mind." It took three years for Roberto to earn enough money to pay for a used bicycle. He enjoyed riding that bicycle because he had worked so hard for it.

The climate is warm all year in Puerto Rico, and it is always comfortable to be outside. So Puerto Rican social life and games take place outdoors. People sit on their porches, playing dominoes and listening to baseball games or music. They have cookouts and outdoor dances. The island's number-one sport is the great outdoor game of baseball.

Baseball was the best part of Roberto Clemente's childhood. "Roberto was born to be a baseball player," his mother said. Each day he ran home from the Fernandez Grammar School, drank a glass of milk, and dashed outside to play.

"He played surprisingly well against boys his age or older," his father said. It seemed that Roberto was never without a ball in his hand. Usually, he had a rubber ball that cost only a few pennies. Sometimes when a ball broke or got lost, Roberto took a few pennies from his jar for another. Sometimes he made a "ball" of crushed magazine pages wrapped in string. Night and day, he had a ball in his hand. He bounced it against walls. He threw it into the air and caught it. He squeezed it, to strengthen his hands and arms. He even kept it next to him in bed at night as he listened to baseball games on the radio.